DRIVE INTO DANGER

Mark Miles has many trucks. They drive all over Europe taking different things to different places.

But today, Mark and his son Andy are having a bad morning. One of their drivers, Gary Slater, has a bad arm and cannot drive. And there are important things to do – some tables must go from England to France, and some wine must come from France to England. But Kim Parker can help – she can drive a truck.

Gary says, 'At about one o'clock, you need to stop for 15 minutes at this truck stop *here*.' He puts an X on the map – he is being *very* helpful.

So Kim drives the truck to France, with Mark's son Andy – but it is a drive into danger . . .

OXFORD BOOKWORMS LIBRARY
Thriller & Adventure

Drive into Danger

Starter (250 headwords)

ROSEMARY BORDER

Drive into Danger

Illustrated by
Simon Gurr

OXFORD UNIVERSITY PRESS

OXFORD
UNIVERSITY PRESS

Great Clarendon Street, Oxford OX2 6DP

Oxford University Press is a department of the University of Oxford.
It furthers the University's objective of excellence in research, scholarship,
and education by publishing worldwide in

Oxford New York

Auckland Cape Town Dar es Salaam Hong Kong Karachi
Kuala Lumpur Madrid Melbourne Mexico City Nairobi
New Delhi Shanghai Taipei Toronto

With offices in

Argentina Austria Brazil Chile Czech Republic France Greece
Guatemala Hungary Italy Japan Poland Portugal Singapore
South Korea Switzerland Thailand Turkey Ukraine Vietnam

OXFORD and OXFORD ENGLISH are registered trade marks of
Oxford University Press in the UK and in certain other countries

ISBN: 978 0 19 423420 7

A complete recording of this Bookworms edition of
Drive into Danger is available on audio CD. ISBN 978 0 19 423402 3

Printed in China

This book is printed on paper from certified and well-managed sources.

Word count (main text): 1440

For more information on the Oxford Bookworms Library, visit
www.oup.com/bookworms

CONTENTS

A TRUCK WITHOUT A DRIVER

Mark Miles and his son Andy are having a bad morning.

'Where's Gary?' says Mark. ' He isn't usually late. The truck is ready. Everybody's waiting.'

Then Gary Slater comes to the office. He is ill. 'I've got a bad arm, Mr Miles,' says Gary. 'I'm very sorry, but I can't drive today.'

1

Just then Kim Parker arrives. She is a student. Her father is one of Mark's drivers. She is working in Mark's office in her holiday.

'Good morning, Mr Miles,' says Kim. 'What can I do first?'

'Can you drive a truck?' says Mark with a little laugh. 'I've got tables in Faversham and wine in Lyon – and no driver!'

'Yes, I can drive a truck,' says Kim. 'I've got a licence.'

'Wonderful!' says Mark. He is looking happier. 'Have you got a passport?'

'Of course. It's at home.' Suddenly Mark is much happier.

'OK. Can you take a truck to France? Here is some French money and these are all the papers – read them carefully.'

'Can I go too, Dad?' asks Andy. 'I can't drive a truck, but I can drive a car and read a map – and I can speak French. Perhaps I can help Kim.'

'And you want to go to France. I know! OK, you two. Run home and get your passports, your overnight bags and some sandwiches. There are sleeping bags in the truck, and a mobile phone too. When you come back, go and look at the map with Gary. He drives to France every week. He can tell you about it.'

'Get the tables from the shop at Faversham,' says Gary. 'Then take the ferry from Dover to Calais. At Calais, look for signs to the A26 motorway. It's a good, fast road.

'Listen – this is very important. All truck drivers *must* stop for 45 minutes in every 4 hours.'

'I know,' says Kim.

'OK. There are truck stops on every French road. At about one o'clock, you need to stop for 15 minutes at this truck stop *here*.' He puts an X on the map.

5

'Don't stay in the truck; get out, walk about and get some coffee. You don't want to go to sleep when you are driving. At about four o'clock you must stop again *here*, near Dijon.' Again Gary puts an X on the map.

'The café at the truck stop makes wonderful coffee. Good luck, and drive carefully,' says Gary.

Andy and Kim get into the truck and drive away – and Gary makes an important phone call.

'Hullo. Gary here. I can't drive today, but tell Paul it's OK – the truck stop near Reims at one, and Dijon at four. Look for a girl with brown hair and a boy in a yellow shirt.'

'THE TRUCK IS LOSING OIL!'

Andy and Kim arrive at Faversham. They tell the man about Gary's arm.

'The tables are ready. My men can put them in the truck. We can sit in my office and wait. Would you like some coffee?' the man says.

They leave the truck and go into the office.

Kim and Andy drive to Dover and take the ferry to Calais. They drive off the ferry, and out of Calais. They find the motorway – and a big STOP sign.

'We need a ticket,' says Andy. He puts his hand out of the window to take the ticket; but he is too far away and the ticket goes under the truck. Andy jumps down and goes to get it.

'OK, I've got it now,' Andy calls to Kim. 'But the truck is losing oil. Not much, but we must do something about it soon.'

'OK,' says Kim. 'I can do that at the truck stop. Come on – let's go!'

They arrive at the truck stop near Reims at about one o'clock. Kim gets under the truck.

'You're right,' she tells Andy. 'The truck *is* losing oil. But it isn't very bad.' Then suddenly she calls to Andy.

'Come and have a look at this.'

There is a box under the truck.

'Is it a sandwich box?' asks Andy. 'Perhaps Gary puts his sandwiches in it.'

'Under a hot, dirty, oily truck?' says Kim. 'Nobody does that! Oh well, I need some coffee.' She goes to the café.

They get into the truck again and drive along the motorway.

'Our next stop is near Dijon,' said Andy. 'Dijon is in Burgundy. They make wonderful wine there.'

'I don't want any wine,' laughs Kim, 'but I do want some coffee.'

They arrive at the truck stop just before four and sit down in the café. Suddenly Andy says, 'Someone's looking under the truck!'

Through the window of the café they see a fat man in a green shirt. He takes something out from under the truck and goes to a red car.

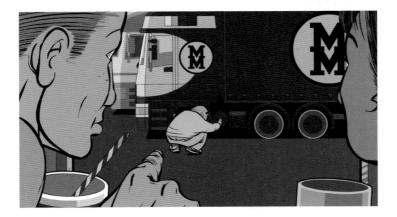

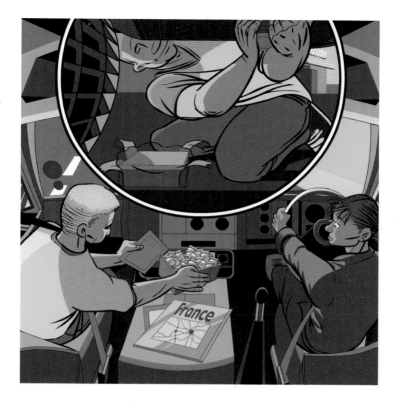

'I don't like this,' says Kim quietly. 'Let's go!'

A few minutes later, Kim looks in her mirror.

'Andy,' she says quietly, 'There's a red car behind us. And the man in the green shirt is driving. Why is he following us? He's got his parcel.'

'No, he hasn't,' says Andy with a laugh. 'He's got our sandwiches. And I've got his parcel. Here it is.'

He opens it carefully. In it are about fifty small white paper bags.

'What's this?' says Andy.

'Drugs, I think,' says Kim. 'And the man in the green shirt wants them. He *doesn't* want your sandwiches, and he's angry. We're in danger, Andy. I must do something.'

The red car is only a few metres behind. Kim stops suddenly. The red car runs into the back of the truck.

Kim drives away again very fast. In her mirror she sees the man in the green shirt standing by his car.

'He can't follow us now,' Andy says with a smile.

But the man is very angry and quickly takes out a small black mobile phone.

'We must leave the motorway,' says Kim.

They take a quiet country road through small villages. Suddenly Andy sees a big sign on their left. 'Go in there!' he says.

'But it's a rubbish dump. Why do you want to go there?' says Kim.

But she drives through the entrance. Andy opens his window and throws the parcel of drugs into the nearest skip.

'We must phone for help,' says Andy.

But just then two men arrive in a white car. A man in a black suit is driving. The man in the green shirt is with him.

The two men leave their car across the entrance and jump out. The man in the suit has a gun.

'Now we can't drive out of here,' thinks Kim. 'Oh dear . . . '

The two men run up to the truck and stand by Kim's door.

'Give me the parcel,' says the man in the black suit very quietly.

'Run, Andy!' says Kim. Quickly Andy opens his door and jumps out of the truck. He runs to the white car. The man in the green shirt follows him, but he is too fat and slow. Andy gets into the car and drives away.

Kim opens her door suddenly. The big mirror hits the man in the suit. He falls down, and loses his gun. Quickly Kim jumps out of the truck and gets the gun.

'Your drugs are in that skip,' she says. 'Go and get them. Take your friend with you.'

The two men go up the ladder and look down into the
skip.

'Go on!' says Kim. 'You want them. Go and look for
them.'

The two men jump down into the skip. Quickly Kim
takes the ladder away. Now the men cannot get out.

Carefully Kim puts the gun in her overnight bag. Then she goes to the truck and telephones the police. A French policeman answers.

'Hullo, do you speak English?' she asks the policeman on the phone.

But Kim does not speak French, and the French policeman does not understand English.

'Where's Andy?' thinks Kim. 'He speaks French.'

Just then a white car comes through the entrance to the rubbish dump. It stops, and Andy jumps out. He runs up to Kim.

'It's OK, Kim,' he says. 'The police are coming.'

A few minutes later a French police car arrives. Four policemen jump out. Kim gives them the gun.

'Where are the drugs?' asks one of the policemen. 'And where are the men?'

'In that skip,' says Andy with a laugh. The policemen get the ladder.

Later that evening Andy and Kim drive to Lyon with the tables. They have coffee and long French sandwiches in a café. Then they go to the wine shop. They arrive very late. A fat, little man is waiting for them. He looks angry.

'Why are you late?' asks the man.

'Well. . .' begins Kim.

'It's a long story,' says Andy tiredly.

GLOSSARY

café a place where people can eat and drink

coffee a hot drink

danger something that can hurt you or get you into trouble

dirty you need to have a bath when you are dirty

drug something that some people take to make them feel happy or sleepy

entrance the way into somewhere

fall go down suddenly

ferry a way of getting cars and trucks across the sea

follow go after

gun something that shoots and kills people

jump move quickly or suddenly

licence you need this paper before you can drive a car

motorway a big road where you can drive fast

oil a liquid that helps cars and trucks move

overnight bag a bag with sleeping and washing things

passport you need this book to travel outside your country

throw move your arm quickly to send something through the air

truck stop a place where trucks stop and their drivers eat and drink

wine an adult drink made from fruit

Drive into Danger

ACTIVITIES

Before Reading

1 **Look at the picture on the cover of the book. Now answer these questions.**

  1 Which word is important for the story? Choose one
     answer.
     a ☐ trucks   b ☐ planes   c ☐ motorbikes
  2 The story is . . .
     a ☐ frightening. b ☐ exciting.   c ☐ funny.

2 **Read the back cover of the book. Guess the answers to these questions.**

  1 The story happens in . . .
     a ☐ America.   b ☐ Britain.   c ☐ France.
  2 The end of the story is . . .
     a ☐ happy.   b ☑ not happy. c ☐ funny.
  3 Kim and Andy. . .
     a ☐ are brother and sister.
     b ☐ are friends.
     c ☐ work together.

While Reading

1 Read pages 1–4.
Are these sentences true (T) or false (F)?   T   F

1 Gary is always late for work.   ☐   ☐
2 Kim is a student.   ☐   ☐
3 Andy is Mark's son.   ☐   ☐
4 Gary does not often drive to France.   ☐   ☐

2 Read pages 5–7, and then put these sentences in the right order.

a ☐ At about four o'clock you must stop near Dijon.

b ☐ At Calais, look for signs to the A16 motorway.

c ☐ You need to stop at about one o'clock.

d ☐ Take the ferry from Dover to Calais.

e ☐ Get the tables from the shop in Faversham.

3 Read pages 8–11. Use these words to join the sentences together.

and   but   because

1 Andy and Kim arrive at Faversham. They tell the man about Gary's arm.

2 The ticket goes under the truck. Andy is too far away to get it.

3 The truck is losing oil. It isn't very bad.

4 **Read pages 12–15.**
  Are these sentences true (T) or false (F)?

		T	F
1	Andy says, 'They make wonderful wine in Burgundy.'	☐	☐
2	A thin man in a black shirt takes something out from under the truck.	☐	☐
3	A red car follows them.	☐	☐
4	The truck runs into the back of the red car.	☐	☑

5 **Read pages 16–21. Who says:**

  1 'We must phone for help.'
  2 'Give me that parcel.'
  3 'Run, Andy!'
  4 'Your drugs are in that skip.'

6 **Read pages 22–24, then answer these questions.**

  1 Where does Kim put the gun?
  2 How do the policemen get into the skip?
  3 What do Kim eat and drink in the café?
  4 Why is the man in the wine shop angry?

After Reading

1 **Here are twenty short sentences. Make ten longer sentences with *and*, *but*, *then* or *because*.**

1 Gary Slater can't drive. He has a bad arm.
2 'Get the tables from Faversham. Take the ferry from Dover to Calais.'
3 Truck drivers must stop every few hours. They must not go to sleep on the road.
4 Kim and Andy drive away. Gary makes an important phone call.
5 Andy has got the ticket. The truck is losing oil.
6 Kim does not want any wine. She does want some coffee.
7 'He's got our sandwiches. I've got his parcel.'
8 Kim stops suddenly. She drives away very fast.
9 Andy opens his window. He throws the parcel into the nearest skip.
10 The man in the green shirt tries to follow Andy. he is too fat and slow.

2 **What are they saying? Write the right answers in the spaces.**

Gary is saying

....

Andy is saying

....

Kim is saying

....

The policeman is saying

....

a 'Why are we going to a rubbish dump?'

b 'Where are the two men?'

c 'OK. You take the ferry from Dover to Calais, then   we drive to Lyon.'

d 'I'm ready. I've got my overnight bag.'

ABOUT THE AUTHOR

Rosemary Border is a very experienced teacher and writer. She has also worked as an editor, a lawyer, and a journalist. She is the author of many books for learners of English – more than she can remember. 'I stopped counting after 150,' she says. She has written and retold more than eighty graded readers, including many for the Oxford Bookworms Library. Among these are *The Fifteenth Character* (Starter, Thriller & Adventure) and *The Lottery Winner* (Stage 1, Human Interest).

OXFORD BOOKWORMS LIBRARY

Classics • Crime & Mystery • Factfiles • Fantasy & Horror
Human Interest • Playscripts • Thriller & Adventure
True Stories • World Stories

The OXFORD BOOKWORMS LIBRARY provides enjoyable reading in English, with a wide range of classic and modern fiction, non-fiction, and plays. It includes original and adapted texts in seven carefully graded language stages, which take learners from beginner to advanced level. An overview is given on the next pages.

All Stage 1 titles are available as audio recordings, as well as over eighty other titles from Starter to Stage 6. All Starters and many titles at Stages 1 to 4 are specially recommended for younger learners. Every Bookworm is illustrated, and Starters and Factfiles have full-colour illustrations.

The OXFORD BOOKWORMS LIBRARY also offers extensive support. Each book contains an introduction to the story, notes about the author, a glossary, and activities. Additional resources include tests and worksheets, and answers for these and for the activities in the books. There is advice on running a class library, using audio recordings, and the many ways of using Oxford Bookworms in reading programmes. Resource materials are available on the website <www.oup.com/bookworms>.

The *Oxford Bookworms Collection* is a series for advanced learners. It consists of volumes of short stories by well-known authors, both classic and modern. Texts are not abridged or adapted in any way, but carefully selected to be accessible to the advanced student.

You can find details and a full list of titles in the *Oxford Bookworms Library Catalogue* and *Oxford English Language Teaching Catalogues*, and on the website <www.oup.com/bookworms>.

THE OXFORD BOOKWORMS LIBRARY
GRADING AND SAMPLE EXTRACTS

STARTER • 250 HEADWORDS

present simple – present continuous – imperative –
can/cannot, must – *going to* (future) – simple gerunds …

Her phone is ringing – but where is it?

Sally gets out of bed and looks in her bag. No phone. She looks under the bed. No phone. Then she looks behind the door. There is her phone. Sally picks up her phone and answers it. ***Sally's Phone***

STAGE 1 • 400 HEADWORDS

… past simple – coordination with *and, but, or* –
subordination with *before, after, when, because, so* …

I knew him in Persia. He was a famous builder and I worked with him there. For a time I was his friend, but not for long. When he came to Paris, I came after him – I wanted to watch him. He was a very clever, very dangerous man. ***The Phantom of the Opera***

STAGE 2 • 700 HEADWORDS

… present perfect – *will* (future) – *(don't) have to, must not, could* –
comparison of adjectives – simple *if* clauses – past continuous –
tag questions – *ask/tell* + infinitive …

While I was writing these words in my diary, I decided what to do. I must try to escape. I shall try to get down the wall outside. The window is high above the ground, but I have to try. I shall take some of the gold with me – if I escape, perhaps it will be helpful later. ***Dracula***

... should, may – present perfect continuous – *used to* – past perfect –
causative – relative clauses – indirect statements ...

Of course, it was most important that no one should see
Colin, Mary, or Dickon entering the secret garden. So Colin
gave orders to the gardeners that they must all keep away
from that part of the garden in future. *The Secret Garden*

STAGE 4 • 1400 HEADWORDS

... past perfect continuous – passive (simple forms) –
would conditional clauses – indirect questions –
relatives with *where/when* – gerunds after prepositions/phrases ...

I was glad. Now Hyde could not show his face to the world
again. If he did, every honest man in London would be
proud to report him to the police. *Dr Jekyll and Mr Hyde*

STAGE 5 • 1800 HEADWORDS

... future continuous – future perfect –
passive (modals, continuous forms) –
would have conditional clauses – modals + perfect infinitive ...

If he had spoken Estella's name, I would have hit him. I was so
angry with him, and so depressed about my future, that I could
not eat the breakfast. Instead I went straight to the old house.
Great Expectations

STAGE 6 • 2500 HEADWORDS

... passive (infinitives, gerunds) – advanced modal meanings –
clauses of concession, condition

When I stepped up to the piano, I was confident. It was as if I
knew that the prodigy side of me really did exist. And when I
started to play, I was so caught up in how lovely I looked that
I didn't worry how I would sound. *The Joy Luck Club*

The Fifteenth Character

ROSEMARY BORDER

'It's an interesting job,' says Sally about her work at Happy Hills. And today is a very exciting day because Zapp the famous singer is coming. Everybody is having a wonderful time. But suddenly something goes wrong – very wrong.

Escape

PHILLIP BURROWS AND MARK FOSTER

'I'm not a thief. I'm an innocent man,' shouts Brown. He is angry because he is in prison and the prison guards hate him. Then one day Brown has an idea. It is dangerous – very dangerous.

Girl on a Motorcycle

JOHN ESCOTT

'Give me the money,' says the robber to the Los Angeles security guard. The guard looks at the gun and hands over the money. The robber has long blond hair and rides a motorcycle – and a girl with long blond hair arrives at Kenny's motel – on a motorcycle. Is she the robber?

Give us the Money

MAEVE CLARKE

'Every day is the same. Nothing exciting ever happens to me,' thinks Adam one boring Monday morning. But today is not the same. When he helps a beautiful young woman because some men want to take her bag, life gets exciting and very, very dangerous.

The Lottery Winner
ROSEMARY BORDER

Everybody wants to win the lottery. A million pounds, perhaps five million, even ten million. How wonderful! Emma Carter buys a ticket for the lottery every week, and puts the ticket carefully in her bag. She is seventy-three years old and does not have much money. She would like to visit her son in Australia, but aeroplane tickets are very expensive.

Jason Williams buys lottery tickets every week too. But he is not a very nice young man. He steals things. He hits old ladies in the street, snatches their bags and runs away . . .

The Wizard of Oz
L.FRANK BAUM
Retold by Rosemary Border

Dorothy lives in Kansas, USA, but one day a cyclone blows her and her house to a strange country called Oz. There, Dorothy makes friends with the Scarecrow, the Tin Man, and the Cowardly Lion.

But she wants to go home to Kansas. Only one person can help her, and that is the country's famous Wizard. So Dorothy and her friends take the yellow brick road to the Emerald City, to find the Wizard of Oz . . .